Finding Shapes

Circles

Diyan Leake

Heinemann Library
Chicago, Illinois

Customer Service 888-454-2279
Visit our website at www.heinemannlibrary.com

Editorial: Diyan Leake
Design: Joanna Hinton-Malivoire
Photo research: Maria Joannou
Production: Chloe Bloom

Library of Congress Cataloging-in-Publication Data
Leake, Diyan.
  Circles / Diyan Leake.
      p. cm. -- (Finding shapes)
  Includes bibliographical references and index.
  ISBN 1-4034-7474-5 (library binding-hardcover : alk. paper) -- ISBN 1-4034-7479-6 (pbk. : alk. paper)
  1. Circle--Juvenile literature. 2. Geometry--Juvenile literature. I. Title. II. Series.

  QA484.L36 2005
  516'.152--dc22

                              2005013852

Printed and bound in China by South China Printing Co. Ltd

10 09 08 07 06
10 9 8 7 6 5 4 3 2 1

Acknowledgments
The author and publishers are grateful to the following for permission to reproduce copyright material: Alamy Images pp. **5**, **14** (Alex Segre), **15** (Andre Jenny), back cover (traffic lights, Alex Segre); Corbis p. **13** (Paul A. Souders), back cover (moon, Paul A. Souders); Harcourt Education Ltd pp. **6** (Malcolm Harris), **7** (Malcolm Harris), **8** (Malcolm Harris), **9** (Malcolm Harris), **10** (Malcolm Harris), **11** (Malcolm Harris), **12** (Malcolm Harris), **17** (Malcolm Harris), **18** (Malcolm Harris), **19** (Tudor Photography), **20** (Malcolm Harris), **21** (Malcolm Harris), **22** (Tudor Photography), **23** (cylinder, Tudor Photography; hollow, Malcolm Harris)

Cover photograph reproduced with the permission of Corbis

Every effort has been made to contact copyright holders of any material reproduced in this book. Any omissions will be rectified in subsequent printings if notice is given to the publishers.

The author and publisher would like to thank Patti Barber, specialist in Early Childhood Education, for her advice and assistance in the preparation of this book.

The paper used to print this book comes from sustainable resources.

Contents

Some words are shown in bold, **like this**. They are explained in the glossary on page 23.

What Is a Circle?

A circle is a **flat**, round shape.

You can see flat shapes but you cannot pick them up.

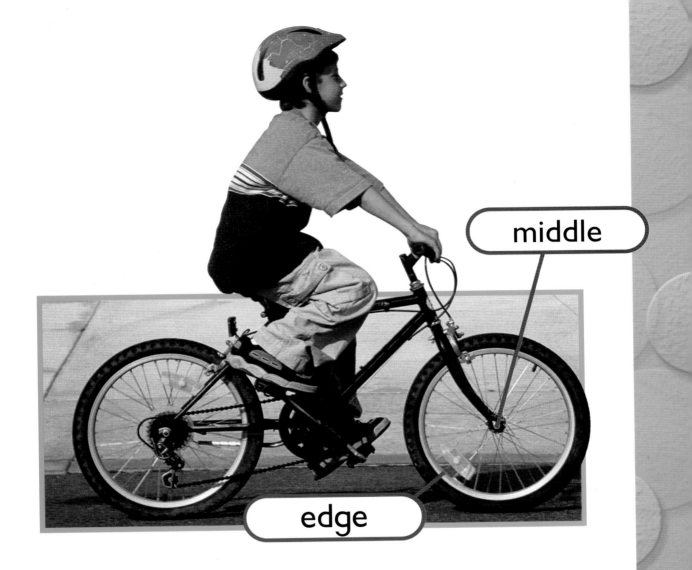

middle

edge

Circles are **curved** all the way around.

They are the same length from the edge to the middle.

Can I See Circles at Home?

There are lots of circles at home.

Some of them are in the living room.

These mugs and bottles have circles on them.

What other circles are there at home?

There are circles in the kitchen.

Plates and some baking pans have a circle shape.

Round fruits and vegetables look like circles when we slice them.

Can I See Circles at School?

There are lots of circles at school.

Some circles are big and some circles are small.

You can see blue circles and yellow circles in this game.

Are there circles outside?

This climber is outside.

You can look through the circles on it.

The full moon is a circle in the sky.

The night sky is not so dark when the moon is full.

Are There Circles in Town?

We can see all sorts of circles in town.

We see a red, yellow, or green circle when we look at traffic lights.

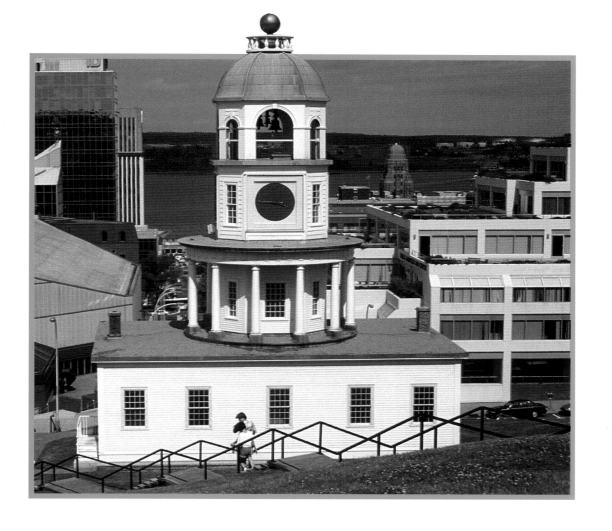

Some buildings have circles
on them.

The clock face on this building
is a circle.

Can Circles Be Part of Other Shapes?

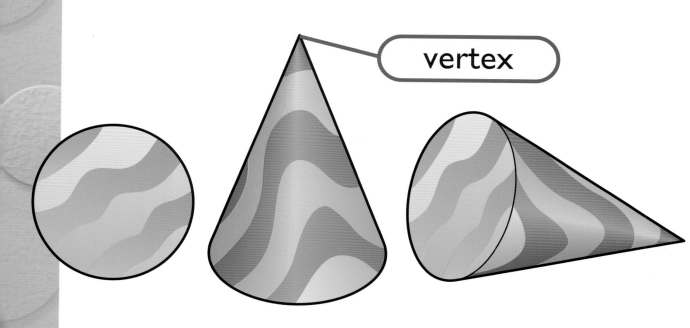

vertex

A **cone** has a circle at one end and a **vertex** at the other.

The vertex is the pointed part of the cone.

These cones are **hollow**, so you can put ice cream in them.

What other cones can you find at a party?

These party hats are **cones**.

A cone does not roll if you put it on its **flat** side.

A **cylinder** has a circle at each end.

Cylinders can be big or small.

Where Can I Find Cylinders?

There are lots of **cylinders** in the kitchen.

These cylinders are shiny.

Cylinders do not roll when they stand on their ends.

They can roll when they are on their sides.

Can I Go on a Circle Hunt?

Walk around the room and see how many circles you can find!

Picture Glossary

cone
shape that has a circle at one end and a pointed vertex at the other

curved
bends; is not straight

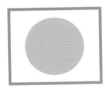
cylinder
shape that has a circle at each end and a curved part in between

flat
having no thickness

hollow
having space inside

vertex
corner of a shape

Index

Note to Parents and Teachers

Reading nonfiction texts for information is an important part of a child's literacy development. Readers can be encouraged to ask simple questions and then use the text to find the answers. Each chapter in this book begins with a question. Read the questions together. Look at the pictures. Talk about what the answer might be. Then read the text to find out if your predictions were correct. To develop readers' inquiry skills, encourage them to think of other questions they might ask about the topic. Discuss where you could find the answers. Assist children in using the contents page, picture glossary, and index to practice research skills and new vocabulary.